STO

St. Pancras
Station

Sadler's
Wells Theatre

N
W E
S

London
University

British
Museum

Liverpool
Street
Station

Theaters

The
Temple

Tower
of
London

ST. JAMES'S
PARK

Royal
Festival
Hall

Old Vic
Theatre

London
Bridge
Station

Waterloo
Station

Westminster
Abbey

Lambeth
Palace

Tate
Gallery

Thames

DOMINE   DIRIGE   NOS

LONDON

The statue of Peter Pan in Kensington Gardens

[CITIES of the WORLD] LONDON

by MAURICE ROSENBAUM

illustrated by ROSEMARY ALDRIDGE

 RAND MᶜNALLY & COMPANY
CHICAGO   NEW YORK   SAN FRANCISCO

For Sarah Lucy

The poem on page 16 is from *Up and Down,* by Walter de la Mare, which is printed with the permission of the literary trustees of Walter de la Mare and The Society of Authors as their representative.

The illustration on page 81 was provided by the Clarke-Hall Bookshop and is used with their permission.

CONTENTS

ILLUSTRATIONS

I.

THE BELLS OF LONDON TOWN

When they hear the name "London," people think of many different things. For some it means royal processions and ceremonies in scarlet and gold, brilliant uniforms, and quaint customs carried over from days long past. Some people think of it mainly as a great port and market for goods from all over the world. For others it is a rather solemn, weather-gray old grandmother of the English-speaking peoples, which they hope to visit at least once.

And to something like ten million Londoners it is home in the simplest sense of all, the immense town, or rather collection of towns, where they live and work.

To many people, too, London is the sound of bells. For such a highly industrialized modern city the chime of bells still plays a surprisingly prominent part in everyday life. Anybody who has ever heard—in the streets of London, or on the radio, or in a movie—the deep voice of Big Ben, the famous bell that booms out the hours from the Clock Tower of the Houses of Parliament in Westminster, will recognize how naturally the very name of the city falls into the pattern of the chime . . . *LONDON*

In the Middle Ages, when England's capital was no more than a maze of narrow streets clustered round Old St. Paul's and London Bridge, there were more than a hundred churches within its narrow bounds, and their bells were already famous. The part they have played in London life over the centuries is proved by the fact that, probably since medieval times, they have been part of the games and folklore of children. One of the best-known English children's play songs begins:

> *Gay go up and gay go down*
> *To ring the bells of London town . . .*

There are many different versions, with lots of verses. Here, for example, are some of them:

> *Oranges and lemons,*
> *Say the bells of St. Clement's.*

> *You owe me five farthings,*
> *Say the bells of St. Martin's.*

> *When will you pay me?*
> *Say the bells of Old Bailey.*

> *When I grow rich,*
> *Say the bells of Shoreditch.*

> *When will that be?*
> *Say the bells of Stepney.*

> *I do not know,*
> *Says the great bell of Bow.*

The "bells of St. Clement's" are those of the church

*Big Ben in the Clock
Tower of the Houses
of Parliament*

of St. Clement Danes, which stands on an island site in the middle of the road at the eastern end of the Strand, near the Law Courts. It was designed by Sir Christopher Wren, the greatest architect England has ever had, and was built in 1681 on the site of an old Danish cemetery. For centuries a special ceremony was held there in March every year at which oranges and lemons were given to English children by the children of Danish residents.

During the air raids of the Second World War the church was so badly damaged that only the external walls were left, and holes caused by the bombs can still be seen in the walls of the Law Courts just across the road. After the war the church was repaired and dedicated to the Royal Air Force, and the bells played the old tune again.

Standing in a tiny patch of garden at the eastern end of St. Clement Danes is a statue of Dr. Samuel Johnson, the great eighteenth-century essayist and dictionary-maker, who was a great lover of London. Dr. Johnson found the London he lived in so interesting that he once wrote: "The man who is tired of London is tired of life."

Most of the bells mentioned in the old rhyme are those of specific churches—St. Clement's, St. Martin's, Stepney Church, Shoreditch Church, and so on. Others are districts of old London where a number of churches are clustered, such as Old Bailey. The "great bell of Bow" refers to the Church of St. Mary-le-Bow, in Cheapside, which not only has one of the most beautiful of all Wren steeples, but is famous because it is the church referred to in the old saying that a true "Cockney"—a real, native-born Londoner —is a person born "within sound of Bow bells."

The church of St. Clement Danes

II.

HOW MANY LONDONS ARE THERE?

Just as London makes different people think of dif-
ferent things, there are many different Londons which go
to make up the vast complex of townships, villages, and
suburbs known as Greater London.

If we start with the very heart, or core, or nucleus
of London, we find an area of 677 acres, or just over a
square mile, in which the city began. This is the "City
of London," also known simply as "the City," or "the
Square Mile," and in it are found St. Paul's Cathedral,
the Mansion House, London Bridge, the Bank of England,
the Royal Exchange, Guildhall, Fleet Street, most of the
Tower of London, and many other famous places.

To the west of the City of London is the City of Westminster. These two, and twenty-seven other metropolitan
boroughs, form an area known as the County of London,
which covers 117 square miles and has a population of just
over three million.

The County of London is surrounded by outer districts, all of which also belong to London, and this vast
area, known as "Greater London," covers 720 square miles,

14

The gryphon monument, Temple Bar, marking the entrance to the city

with a total population of nearly ten million. (See endpaper map.)

The government of such a huge and complicated collection of districts is no small problem, and many proposals have been made for simplifying the control of public services and local authorities throughout the area. Foremost among these is a plan for revising the role of the London County Council, the body that governs the County of London.

The City of London began on the north bank of the Thames near London Bridge; Westminster grew up to the west as the center of national government. The City of London's western boundary falls where Fleet Street runs into the Strand. There, in the middle of the already narrow roadway near St. Clement Danes and the Law Courts, there is a curious monument with an even more curious winged animal—called a gryphon—on top.

15

This marks the place where Temple Bar used to stand —an ancient stone gateway between the City of London and the City of Westminster. The gateway has long been removed to make more room—but there is still very little room—for traffic. It is preserved in the grounds of a great country house outside London, although there is talk of bringing it back to some convenient site in the City.

Meanwhile the gryphon still marks the place where Temple Bar stood, and guards the entrance to the City. The tradition of the City's independence is still so strong that when the Sovereign visits the City on State occasions, the ancient custom of obtaining the Lord Mayor's permission to "pass Temple Bar" is still observed.

Walter de la Mare, one of the favorite poets of English children, wrote:

> *Down the Hill of Ludgate*
> *Up the Hill of Fleet,*
> *To and fro and East and West*
> *With people flows the street;*
> *Even the King of England*
> *On Temple Bar must beat*
> *For leave to ride to Ludgate*
> *Down the Hill of Fleet.*

A wooden gateway is known to have been on this spot in 1502, and some kind of bar or chain was drawn across the road as long ago as the twelfth century. The Temple Bar that is preserved is another example of Sir Christopher Wren's architecture. It was built in 1672, after the Great Fire of London of 1666.

Westminster Abbey

The beginning of London—the first Roman settlements —was in what is now the City itself. Westminster, on the other hand, is the royal city. It contains Buckingham Palace, the official residence of the Sovereign; St. James's Palace, the Court to which all the ambassadors of foreign countries are accredited; the Houses of Parliament, government offices, beautiful parks, the best-known shopping streets, theaters, hotels, restaurants and, of course, Westminster Abbey, where the kings and queens of England are married and crowned, and many of them buried, although the Georges of the present Windsor dynasty are

Coronation chair, Westminster Abbey

St. James's Palace

buried at Windsor. Kensington Palace, which provides homes for members or relatives of the royal family, and also houses the London Museum, is just over the border in the Royal Borough of Kensington.

In addition to the City itself and that part of Westminster where the Houses of Parliament, the government offices, and Westminster Abbey are, there are other parts of central London which have their own essential character: Soho, with its cosmopolitan shops and restaurants; Mayfair, with its luxurious apartment houses and hotels; Bloomsbury, with its atmosphere of study and literature and its fine squares in the area near London University and the British Museum; the calm elegance of St. James's, with its royal palace, and park, and aristocratic clubs; Piccadilly, with its shops, arcades, hotels, and night life; Chelsea, which has something in common with New York's Greenwich Village and Paris's Latin Quarter, but at the same time is in some ways as quiet and detached from the main stream of London life as the riverside village it once was; and Whitehall, with its government offices, mounted sentries in plumes and breastplates, and that magnificent setting for ceremonial occasions, the Horse Guards Parade.

The Regent's Park district is in the northwest of what is still really central London, if we compare it with the surrounding suburbs of Greater London. It is famous not only for its beautiful park—which contains London's Zoo and a fine rose garden, as well as a lake and lots of playing fields—but also for the terraces of elegant houses surrounding the park. These terraces, designed by the eighteenth-century architect, Beau Nash, are carried out in stucco. This means that the brick buildings, which are well proportioned, are finished off in simple classical designs with

One of the terraces in Regent's Park

a surface of smooth cream plaster, and are planned in groups and blocks to create the most attractive street landscapes when they are seen in relation to the green lawns and fine trees of the park.

Many people think that this is one of the most pleasing and successful methods of designing city streets that has ever been invented; certainly the great Regent's Park terraces, and smaller examples of the same kind of design in South Kensington, and in part of Charing Cross Hospital, opposite Charing Cross railway station, show how charming these smooth, classical frontages can be.

Near Regent's Park, in the borough of St. Marylebone, is an area generally called by the name of its principal street, Harley Street. This includes Wimpole Street—famous as the home of Elizabeth Barrett, before she married the poet Robert Browning—Weymouth Street, and many other adjoining streets and squares, and is almost entirely devoted to medical and dental specialists' offices. It would not be altogether true to say that this is London's "doctors' district," because in London, as in all other cities, doctors live and work where their patients are—that is, spread all over the town—but it is a district devoted to those doctors and dentists who have specialized in particular health problems or diseases, and who, as a rule, can be consulted only if the patient is sent to them by his general physician. It is, appropriately, a district of comparatively quiet streets and dignified private houses converted into "consulting rooms" and nursing homes, with a few small specialized hospitals and a big, modern, fashionable clinic.

Some of London's districts have kept their special char-

20

Eros statue in Piccadilly Circus

acter for centuries; others have changed or even disappeared. Here again the bombing raids of the Second World War have been a powerful factor in changing the face and character of London. The visitor who forgets this will be surprised and disappointed, just as people who have seen *My Fair Lady* may be disappointed to find that there are very few flower girls left in London, and none at all sitting, as they used to do, round the base of the Eros statue in Piccadilly Circus.

The bombing not only destroyed great areas—particularly between the City and the docks in the east—but also led to a permanent redistribution of groups that were formerly concentrated in colorful special districts. There is little left, for example, of the Limehouse that was famous even thirty years ago as London's Chinatown. The Jewish East End, which began at Aldgate—one of the eastern gates of the ancient city of London—and continued eastward to Mile End, has lost much of its old character, although the Sunday morning market in Middlesex Street —familiarly known as "Petticoat Lane"—is still worth a visit, and there is still a street market in puppies in Club Row.

Much of the property that has gone from the old, crowded districts east and northeast of the City of London where poor Jewish, Italian, or Irish people used to live, can only be described as a "good riddance." The fine, new blocks of apartment houses with open spaces, or, as in Poplar, wholly replanned new areas, are a great improvement. But those whose ideas of London come from pre-war

Petticoat Lane, the Sunday morning market

books and plays must be prepared for disappointments.

Although there are still Jewish communities in the East End, and Italians in Saffron Hill, Clerkenwell, and Cypriots in Camden Town, these are no longer the main centers for these groups. Soho is still the most cosmopolitan of all London districts, but there are many French and Italians in the South Kensington district; German-speaking refugees in the Belsize Park area of Hampstead; Indians and Pakistanis in Bloomsbury, South Kensington, Hampstead, and south London, and Chinese restaurants and Italian coffee-bars distributed more or less evenly throughout central London.

One very interesting point about the division of rich and poor in London is that it is only in the outer suburbs and districts that we find communities, either rich or poor, where practically everybody in the particular district is in more or less the same income group. In central London the people living in any district are much more mixed than that. Mayfair, Belgravia, parts of Chelsea and Kensington, St. John's Wood, Knightsbridge, Regent's Park are favored by the well-to-do, but in all of them rich and poor are mixed and great houses rub shoulders with streets of little cottages, tiny general stores, junk shops, and even one or two surviving blacksmiths. Often behind the great houses the former stables or "mews" have been converted into little houses; some of these are quite smart and expensive, others are still occupied by working families who have been there for generations.

In Belgravia, for example, not far from Chelsea's fashionable and rather French-looking Sloane Square, there

23

is a row of cottages called Chester Row. Hidden away behind a wall with an archway in it, these half dozen tiny houses face each other across little gardens and a narrow dividing path that doesn't lead anywhere. It is like a forgotten village. There are many survivals of this sort hidden away in London, but how much longer they will be allowed to go on surviving no one knows.

In the meantime, as a writer on London once said: "In London the very poor and the very rich alone have the privilege of living quite close to the center of their activities."

The Thames River tends to be overlooked in spite of its vital role in London's history. At intervals it is rediscovered and attempts are made to restore its former popularity as the center of London's attractions. One reason for its being overlooked is that it divides London, instead of unifying it. Practically every place of historic importance is on the north or left bank, unlike Paris, where both sides of the Seine are of equal interest.

Both the City of London and Westminster are on the north side of the Thames, as well as about ninety per cent of all the other showplaces and principal buildings of the center of the capital. So are practically all the art and entertainment, the fine shops, the great hotels, the royal parks and palaces—even Covent Garden, the great central market. This means of course that the north bank is the main attraction for all the visitors and most of the foreign residents, and this means, too, that the north bank has the cosmopolitan districts.

Lambeth Palace

On the south bank, Southwark Cathedral, Lambeth Palace—the London home of the Archbishop of Canterbury—and, a few miles down-river, Greenwich, with its Royal Naval College, National Maritime Museum, and riverside park, are the main attractions for the visitor who can spend only a week or so in London. But his sightseeing is almost entirely devoted to the districts occupied by royalty, the Government, the luxury shops, the museums, the colleges, and most of the theater and concert halls on the north bank.

There are exceptions, of course, and they are particularly interesting. The native Londoner and the long-term resident both know that the south side of the river, because of its lack of cosmopolitan attractions, has kept a sort of "ordinary London" quality. Some people think that the only true Londoners live on the south side, since an enormously high proportion of the people who live north of the Thames came originally from other parts of Britain or from abroad.

This "London quality" is emphasized by the fact that the headquarters of the London County Council are on the south bank, and in recent years there have been moves to develop the attractions of that side of the Thames. London's finest concert hall, the Royal Festival Hall, was built on the south side for the Festival of Britain in 1951, and at the same time part of Battersea Park was converted into a fun-fair and pleasure gardens.

One of the sights of London is the huge crowd that pours over London Bridge, Waterloo Bridge, and other

The Royal Festival Hall

bridges in the morning from the south side on their way to work in the City or the West End.

This difference between north and south London is one of the first things we notice in a brief roof-top survey of the British capital. We also notice that there are very few really wide streets with planned vistas. The Mall, which leads from Trafalgar Square to Buckingham Palace, is magnificent; the long view down Whitehall from Trafalgar Square to the Houses of Parliament is impressive, and there are many fine groupings of buildings as we travel around, but most of the memorable glimpses are not the result of planning. It is simply the way London has grown over the centuries.

Everywhere little streets of small or comparatively small houses help to set off great public buildings, so that the eye is constantly refreshed with variety and with relief from the strain of seeing only enormous structures.

There are very few places in central London where we cannot see trees—if not from where we are standing, then by merely walking to the next street corner. As the great red double-decker buses swing around Trafalgar Square, or along the King's Road, Chelsea, or in many other parts of London in the spring or summer, the branches of trees scrape the bus top.

There are almost no outdoor refreshment places in the streets. For one thing, most of London's sidewalks are too narrow for café terraces, even when the weather is fine enough. Instead London has hundreds of small, cozy, indoor eating places, some of them very old-fashioned and snug.

27

The Cheshire Cheese

The spread of medium-priced foreign restaurants is typical of the post-war changes. At one time it was necessary to go to Soho or Limehouse for Chinese food; for French food to Soho; for Italian food to Soho or Saffron Hill, and for Asian food to the East End. Now such restaurants are widespread. On the other hand, London has never been as celebrated as Paris or New York for its special restaurants, and the best known, such as Prunier's, are foreign. The most famous hotels, of course—the Ritz, the Savoy, the Berkeley, Claridges, and so on—are justly celebrated for their cuisine, but in this respect London is no different from Paris or New York.

On the other hand there are still a few specifically English restaurants which the visitor who wants to enjoy English cooking at its best—and it can be superb!—should not miss. Such are Simpson's in the Strand, for magnificent steaks; Simpson's in the city, for fish; Wheeler's oyster bars and restaurants; the Cheshire Cheese, in Wine Office Court, Fleet Street; and quite a number of old English chop-houses in the West End and the City. For those who like to lunch in the company of the stars of the London theater, the Ivy, in West Street, off Charing Cross Road, is a *must*, and Lyons' tea shops and Corner Houses still play a big part in the lives of Londoners and their visitors.

Apart from the fascinating small shops to be seen almost everywhere, one of the most exciting glimpses is that of big, green, open spaces in the very center of London; sheep can sometimes be seen grazing on the remoter slopes of Hyde Park, near Kensington Gardens.

At the Marble Arch corner of Hyde Park crowds gather every week end to hear the speakers who climb up on little wooden platforms and are free to talk about anything under the sun to anybody who cares to stop and listen. They are forbidden only to create a disturbance or to collect money within the park gates.

At the southeast corner of Hyde Park there is a particularly interesting example of the persistence of tradition in London. Where Piccadilly climbs a slope to meet the re-designed huge traffic junction of Hyde Park Corner,

Speaker at the Marble Arch corner of Hyde Park

amidst all the road-widening and tunneling, a curious old shelf, standing on two shoulder-high legs, has been allowed to remain on the edge of the sidewalk.

This is called a fardel-rest, from an old word meaning a burden (Shakespeare wrote about bearing "fardels," and "fardeau" still is in use in modern French), and it was first put there long, long ago so that porters, humping heavy loads up the hill on their backs, could rest them on the shelf, without having to lower them to the ground.

What else do we notice in this preliminary trip? We see railway bridges crossing central London streets, such as the one at the foot of Ludgate Hill, in front of St. Paul's Cathedral. If we stand on the north side of Fleet Street, by the *Daily Telegraph* building, and look toward St. Paul's we see one of the best-known and perhaps one of the most characteristic of all London views.

Ludgate Hill, ancient and still narrow, climbs and winds up to St. Paul's. Post-war reconstruction has added impressive new steel and concrete blocks to the view on the side of the hill between St. Paul's and the Central Criminal Court—the "Old Bailey" of the song mentioned earlier—but the old iron railway bridge that crosses Ludgate Hill remains unchanged. And from time to time steam trains and freight trains chug and clank backward and forward on the bridge, blowing puffs of smoke in the face of St. Paul's.

We notice an extraordinary variety of uniforms in London, from those of soldiers, police, bank-messengers, porters, street-cleaners, officials of the Stock Exchange (who are called "waiters"), commissionaires, government

View from Fleet Street, looking toward St. Paul's Cathedral

messengers, and policewomen, to the "uniform" of the man who is "something in the City"—the dark suit, bowler hat, and tightly rolled umbrella.

And as London is only fifty miles from the sea—Brighton, the nearest point on the south coast is sometimes called London-on-Sea—many workers commute from the seaside by the high-speed electric train service. Thousands of others, pouring in from the suburbs and the nearer countryside by car, bus, and train have helped to create the kind of traffic problem that is now familiar in all the world's great cities.

What else do we see in this "helicopter-view" of London? In the narrow side streets of Chelsea and other old villages that have been swallowed by the metropolis we

Cheyne Walk, in Chelsea

Tying post in Chelsea

see tying-posts on the edge of the sidewalk. Some of these were made from the barrels of cannons captured in the old wars. Originally they were hitching-posts for horses; now children play leap-frog over them. Sometimes we find them in the middle of the tiny alleys or "walks" that link one old side street with another. They were left there to prevent carriages, and later, automobiles, from using the shortcut. And everywhere along the river, even at the busiest parts of it, we see the gliding beauty of white swans.

We also see the French onion-boys who come to London every year from Britanny across the Channel, with huge strings of onions slung on their bicycles. We may even see, in quiet streets where there are children, the age-old Punch and Judy show being performed by a man inside a kind of tall booth. And in the entertainment district of the West End there are still singers, acrobats, dancers, and actors who perform in the street for the amusement of the people on line at theater entrances. These street musicians and entertainers are called "buskers." (See next page.)

Buskers

Even in this brief preliminary glance we have seen enough to realize that London is not only a collection of quaint customs and odd corners, a sort of glorified antique shop. It has, as well, one of the swiftest, best-lighted—and cleanest—underground railway systems in the world, and some of the finest modern shops and stores.

It has so much open space in the heart of the city that you can walk all day in St. James's Park, the Green Park, Hyde Park, and Kensington Gardens and still be within easy reach of Piccadilly, Knightsbridge, Whitehall, or Trafalgar Square. When we get to know it well we find that it tends to absorb what is good in the new and to preserve what is good in the old.

London began on the Thames, or as seafaring men call it, London River. But that is, in itself, so wide and deep a subject, with so many twists and turns, and so much history, that it deserves a chapter of its own.

III.

LONDON RIVER

The Thames River has a special character of its own.
It is not as picturesque as the Seine in Paris, or as much a
seaway as the Hudson or the East River in New York.
Every visitor to Paris notices at once that the center of
the city seems to turn toward the Seine, and the beautiful
riverside walks are among the first pleasures of Paris he
discovers. But the first impression of the newcomer to
London is that the city turns away from the Thames, except in a few places.

It is possible, for example to come into London from
the north, to stay on the northern side of the Thames, and
to leave again, without ever really noticing the river.

There are two main reasons why, in modern times,
London seems to have neglected the possibilities of the riverside as a place of beauty and recreation. One is that London became such a tremendously important place for
world trade and business that wharfs and warehouses had
to be built along the riverside even if it meant building
over the pleasant walks of olden times. The other reason is
that the Thames is tidal, with a great difference in the level

A Thames River fair on the ice,

of the river at high or low tide during certain times and seasons. This has sometimes led to serious flooding in the past, and it has made it necessary to construct the embankments for protection and defense rather than pleasure.

But there was a time, before the "Industrial Revolution" in Britain made the use of iron, steel, and coal for manufacturing seem more important than agriculture, when the river was the center of London's pageantry and splendor. In this period, from the Middle Ages to the latter part of the eighteenth century, royal processions by boat, great fairs on the ice when the river froze, music, fireworks, entertainments, and spectacles of all kinds brought Londoners flocking to the riverside.

This was the time when the author of a book on Lon-

in eighteenth-century London

don, writing in the seventeenth century could say: ". . .
the most glorious sight in the world (take water and
land together) was to come upon a high tide from Gravesend, and shoot the [London] Bridge to Westminster."

Many visitors are surprised when, riding along Whitehall or the Strand on the top deck of a bus, they suddenly
catch a glimpse of the river at the end of a narrow street.
And although a river trip is essential to see London prop-
erly, it is rarely the first thing a visitor discovers. Never-
theless, sooner or later, the visitor will come to realize the
truth of the saying that London "was made by the river,
which many forget, and still is fed by its shipping, which
most Londoners never see."

This first impression of a neglected river is only partly

37

true. There is a fine embankment on the north side of the Thames between Chelsea and Blackfriars. On the south side there is a pleasant terrace in front of St. Thomas's Hospital, with a magnificent view of the Houses of Parliament across the river. And there are also the terraces in front of the Royal Festival Hall.

Farther down the river, toward the sea, there is the pier and waterfront promenade at Greenwich, and going up river into the Thames valley there are delightful riverside walks at Putney, Richmond, and elsewhere.

But before we make a trip down the river to see London, let us first make a little trip backward in time.

In the earliest times of which it is possible to build up an accurate picture, where London now stands the river flowed through deep ravines and swamps, in which lived primitive animals and very primitive human beings, not far removed from the earliest cavemen. Lifelike models of the Thames valley as it must have been in those far-off days can be seen in the Geological Museum.

The history of the London we know today began nearly two thousand years ago, when the Romans, marching from their landing places on the south coast to set up camps on the sites which became Colchester (about 50 miles northeast of London), Chester (184 miles northwest of London), and other English towns, crossed the Thames at a point not very far from where London Bridge now stands.

The Roman bridge was guarded by a strong fortress on the northern side of the river, probably facing a camp set

*Statue of Boadicea
in her chariot*

up by the Britons on the opposite bank of a tributary of the Thames, the Walbrook. Eventually a town grew up at this place, and was enclosed by a Roman wall, fragments of which can be seen in London to this day.

The first reference to London in any history book is probably the one in the records kept by the Roman writer Tacitus, in A.D. 61, when he wrote that the city was remarkable for its great crowds of merchants and its commerce.

A.D. 61 was the year when a tribe of Britons, the Iceni, led by their queen, Boadicea—or Boudicca, as the Romans called her—attacked Roman-occupied London and set fire to it. There is a statue of the war-like Boadicea, in her chariot, at the northern end of Westminster Bridge, facing the Houses of Parliament.

And for those who like to see how history in one part of the world fits in with the history of other countries, it is interesting to recall that Boadicea's fierce revolt against Roman London took place about nine years before the Roman Emperor Titus destroyed Jerusalem, drove the Jews into exile, and ran the plough over the site of the Holy City.

But let us now see what London looks like today by

making an armchair trip down the river from Putney, where the Thames may be said to enter central London, to Greenwich, the last great London landmark before the river reaches the Thames estuary and the sea.

First we must remember that the tidal rise and fall of the Thames, and its swift, strong currents, have always made it impractical to run regular, scheduled "water-bus" services between Putney and Greenwich. During the summer months, however, many pleasure boats make short and long trips so that there are plenty of opportunities for the holiday visitor to see the city from the river. When water-buses sailed from Putney to Greenwich more or less regularly about ten years ago, the average time for the trip was about an hour and a quarter. Today the best way to make the trip is to walk, or drive, along the riverside from Putney to Westminster Pier (about four miles), and then, from Westminster Pier to Greenwich by Thames launch (about three-quarters of an hour).

Putney Pier, a few yards upriver from Putney Bridge, is a good place to start from. The south bank of the river is lined with the boathouses of rowing clubs, for this is where the annual race between the rowing "eights" of the Universities of Oxford and Cambridge begins. But the university boats race upriver toward the open country, and we shall pass under Putney Bridge and head downstream toward the city. And although the river winds so much that sometimes it flows from west to east, and sometimes from south to north, or even north to south, it will be less confusing, as we sail toward the sea, if we call the left bank north, and the right bank south, all the way.

The houseboat community on the Thames

There is a mixture of wharfs, houses, small parks, recreation grounds, and industrial plants on both banks until we enter the stretch of river that lies between Chelsea, on the north, or left, bank, and Battersea on the south. The Battersea side, with its riverside park, pleasure gardens, and fun fair, is a refreshing patch of greenery by day and a twinkling of colored lights by night. The Chelsea side, as befits an old riverside village, is full of charm and interest.

To begin with, just by Battersea Bridge, there is a whole community of people living on the river in houseboats—converted naval craft, and other small vessels—moored to the embankment at the western end of Chelsea's famous Cheyne Walk (see picture on page 32.) Seen from the embankment, from the bridge, from the tiny stretch of "beach" that is exposed at low tide, or from the river itself, this cluster of boats is one of the most picturesque sights in London.

41

The boats are moored shoulder-to-shoulder on both sides of a big boat that serves as the central administrative offices of the river community. This is the only boat that has a gangway to the embankment. To reach any of the other boats means a trip along planks and catwalks from deck to deck on the river side of boat town, so it is easy to imagine what fun it is for children who live in the boats, and for their friends who visit them.

The boat community grew most rapidly just after the Second World War, when people whose homes had been destroyed by bombs found shelter in these floating houses—floating, that is, only at high tide. When the tide is out the houseboats squat in the mud. But nowadays smart and fashionably furnished living rooms show that some, at least, of today's boat residents are movie and theater people, and successful writers.

Then there is Chelsea Old Church, founded in the twelfth century, but mainly associated with Sir Thomas More, who was beheaded in 1535 for refusing to recognize Henry VIII's claim to be supreme head of the English Church, and was declared a saint by the Roman Catholic Church four hundred years later—in 1935. The old church with the square tower, most of which had been extensively rebuilt in the late seventeenth century, was almost entirely destroyed by bombs, and has been restored almost exactly as it was before the last war.

Beyond the next bridge—a handsome suspension bridge named after Queen Victoria's husband, Prince Albert—Chelsea Embankment begins, and from the river can be seen the wrought-iron gates of the Chelsea Physic Garden

—or Physick Garden, as it is sometimes spelled—which is also known as the Apothecaries' Garden.

This garden, which is used by students for research in botany, was established in 1676 on a site given by Sir Hans Sloane (1660-1753), a physician, on condition that 2,000 specimens of distinct plants grown there should be supplied, in annual instalments of 50, to the Royal Society, Britain's leading association of scientists.

Sir Hans, whose statue can be seen in the middle of the garden, was also the creator of the great British Museum, which grew out of his collections of objects of historical and artistic interest. His name is commemorated in Chelsea in Sloane Square, Sloane Street, Sloane Avenue, and Hans Place.

The Physic Garden is notable for its links with America. In the eighteenth century there was an extensive ex-

The Chelsea Physic Garden, with statue of Sir Hans Sloane

change of plants between Philip Miller, curator of the garden, and John Bartram, botanist to George III, who lived in Philadelphia.

From America came birds' nests, tortoises, turtles, and specimens of the nests of bees, wasps, and hornets, while the London garden sent vines, nectars, and 69 varieties of seeds. It was from this garden that the apothecaries sent to John Edward Oglethorpe (1696-1785), the founder of Georgia, cotton seed that helped to establish the cotton industry in America. Oglethorpe, incidentally, was baptized in St. Martin-in-the-Fields, Trafalgar Square.

A little farther on is the Royal Hospital, Chelsea, known also as Chelsea Hospital, or "the Pensioners' Hospital." This group of buildings, built by Sir Christopher Wren between 1682 and 1692, is not a "hospital" in the modern sense, but rather a hostel and club for old and disabled soldiers. It was founded by Charles II, and there is a pleasant legend that the idea was suggested to him by his friend Nell Gwynn, the actress. It is much more likely that the originator of the scheme was Sir Stephen Fox, Paymaster-General of the British Army in Charles II's day.

The "Chelsea Pensioners" are a familiar sight in the district. In winter they wear old-fashioned dark-blue uniforms with peaked caps bearing the letters "R.H." for Royal Hospital. In summer they wear scarlet coats, and make a fine splash of color in the King's Road, which is Chelsea's main street. Among them are still some survivors of wars even earlier than the First World War of 1914-1918. On very special occasions they wear handsome, three-cornered hats with their scarlet coats.

The spacious grounds are the setting for the annual Chelsea Flower Show, and include Ranelagh Gardens. This is a tiny park that belongs to the pensioners but is open to the public with certain restrictions, and usually has a sergeant from the Royal Hospital on duty at the gate. Because it is so little known, and well protected, it is something of a bird sanctuary, and has a great variety of trees.

The stretch of river that runs past the Physic Garden and the Royal Hospital on the north bank, and Battersea Park on the south, is known as Chelsea Reach, and it brings us to Chelsea Bridge. Beyond the bridge, the most striking building on the south side is Battersea Power Station, a fine example of an industrial building designed to have visual grandeur as well as efficiency.

After Chelsea the Thames flows under Vauxhall Bridge and through Westminster, one of the historic twin cities

Lots Road Power Station, Chelsea

that form the heart of London. Here, by the riverside, are the Tate Gallery, containing one of the finest collections of modern art in Europe, and, on the opposite bank, beyond Lambeth Bridge, the warm, red brickwork of Lambeth Palace, the London residence of the Archbishops of Canterbury for the past seven hundred years. The building was begun early in the thirteenth century, and has been constantly added to or altered ever since then. (See picture, page 25.)

Facing Lambeth Palace, on the opposite bank, are, first the terrace gardens, and then the buildings of the Houses of Parliament.

So successfully did the architect, Sir Charles Barry, design these Parliament buildings in the style of the great age of English Gothic that it is always a surprise to learn that, except for Westminster Hall, which is one of the oldest treasures of English architecture and history, they were completed little more than a hundred years ago.

At Westminster Bridge begins one of the most exciting stretches of the river, with so much to see that it is hard work keeping our eyes on both banks. The great sweep and curves of the Thames make the skyline change dramatically as we edge our way toward the sea; great towers and buildings seem to swing round and regroup themselves, while, now on our right, now straight ahead, the majestic dome of St. Paul's Cathedral crowns the view.

But the centuries-old pattern of the skyline is also changing rapidly under the pressure of new building. Before we reached the Houses of Parliament we saw how London's tallest office building, the Vickers, already outtops and overshadows the complex of religious and governmental buildings that is the heart of Westminster; beyond Westminster Bridge, the new Shell Building, on the south bank, similarly throws the rest of traditional London out of scale.

On the south bank is County Hall, headquarters of the London County Council, the governing body of the County of London; on the north bank pleasant gardens run parallel to the Strand, and there is also Scotland Yard, headquarters of the police; on the south bank again is the Royal Festival Hall (see picture, page 26); and, linking the two banks, Charing Cross Railway bridge, which has, running alongside it, Hungerford Foot Bridge, a high-level river crossing for pedestrians from which some of the finest views in London can be obtained while the electric trains rumble along the adjoining tracks.

Ahead are the long, low, white arches of Waterloo Bridge, spread like a seagull's wings over the broad gray river. At low tide a good deal of the water-stained piers or supports of the bridge is exposed, and the proportions of the spans are not then seen at their best, but there is a time between low and high water when those white wings, poised just above the surface of the river against London's gray background, make one of the finest townscapes in the world.

Along this stretch of the Thames, over which broods the majesty of St. Paul's, are, on the north bank, Somerset House, a handsome eighteenth-century building in which all Britain's records of births, marriages, and deaths are kept, and the gardens of the Temple, the wonderfully well-kept

The Temple, and a barrister

grounds of the headquarters of the English Bar. It was in these gardens, the legend says, that the white and red roses were plucked which became the emblems of York and Lancaster in England's "War of the Roses" five hundred years ago. Shakespeare dramatizes this legend in Henry VI.

The Temple—which many visitors miss because it is tucked away between very busy Fleet Street, where most of the principal newspaper offices are, and the river—is one of the most interesting and pleasant of all London's attractions.

The ancient round church and some adjoining buildings belonged, about the year 1160, to the Knights Templars, the crusading knights who took their name from Solomon's Temple in Jerusalem. In the fourteenth century the property was leased to a body of lawyers.

In England the profession of the law is divided into two distinct branches. Members of the Bar, or barristers, who wear the traditional gown, short wig, and white neck-tie with flowing ends, called "bandelettes," plead on behalf of their clients in the High Court and the County Courts. They are not allowed to seek business, but must wait until their services are sought by solicitors—the other branch of the profession—who have been directly approached by the people who wish to bring, or defend, a lawsuit.

For hundreds of years the barristers have had their offices (called chambers), their libraries, their dining halls, and often their apartments in collegiate groups of old buildings with courtyards and gardens known as the "Inns of Court." Of these, the Temple, Lincoln's Inn, and Gray's Inn still survive; others, such as Furnival's Inn, Sergeant's Inn, Staple Inn, and Clement's Inn, are now only the names of streets or old corners of London. Staple Inn, in Holborn, has been preserved with a magnificent half-timbered frontage on the main shopping street.

The Temple, then, is one of these Inns, and although much was destroyed or damaged during the war, it has been so skillfully restored that a walk through its courtyards and alleys is still a great pleasure, like finding the quiet and beauty of an ancient university in the middle of London's noise and bustle.

In this part of the river, too, are the Thames Police Station, headquarters of the river police, on Waterloo Pier, and four ships moored alongside the northern embankment —*Discovery*, *Wellington*, *Chrysanthemum*, and *President*. *Discovery* is the ship in which Captain Scott, the British explorer, made one of his voyages to the Antarctic in 1901; *Wellington* is headquarters of the Honourable Com-

The new Mermaid Theatre

pany of Master Mariners, and *President* and *Chrysanthemum* are training ships of the Royal Naval Volunteer Reserve.

The next part of our voyage of discovery takes us through King's Reach under Blackfriars and Southwark Bridges, and we are now under the shadow of St. Paul's.

This is mainly a riverside of wharfs and industrial buildings—except for the adventurous new Mermaid Theatre on a north bank wharf called Puddle Dock—but a glimpse of the tower of Southwark Cathedral, on the south bank, is a reminder not only that William Shakespeare's younger brother, Edmund, is buried there, but also that this is the church where John Harvard, founder of Harvard University, who was born in the parish, was baptized in 1607.

Southwark Cathedral, a survival of medieval Southwark, has a Harvard Memorial Chapel. When this chapel was being restored and decorated in 1907, an arch dating from Norman times was uncovered, and a fragment of twelfth-century sculpture from it was sent to Harvard University, where it is now in the Appleton Chapel.

The next bridge is London Bridge, near the site where London began. In fact, from the first settlement of London, here, or near here, this was the city's only bridge right up to 1749, when a second bridge was completed at Westminster.

The first London Bridge was built about 994, of wood, and the first stone bridge was completed in 1209. In the seventeenth century it was covered with houses and shops —like the Ponte Vecchio, or Old Bridge, in Florence, Italy, which still survives—and, curiously enough, London's Great Fire of 1666 did little damage to the houses on the bridge. The present bridge was opened by King William IV and Queen Adelaide in 1831.

Between London Bridge and Tower Bridge is the Upper Pool, where a number of freighters are usually to be seen moored opposite the Tower of London. The Tower, which was begun by William the Conqueror to guard and control the city, contains, in the White Tower, the finest Norman "keep" or stronghold in Britain.

This is, of course, one of the most interesting of all the world-famous showplaces of London. Even if only glimpsed from the river it is seen as a wonderful medieval fortress, with its towers and great gates, walls, bastions, courtyards, and moat. Here are the Traitors' Gate and Bloody Tower, the great armory and the Crown Jewels, the Yeomen Warders (sometimes known as "Beefeaters") in their picturesque uniforms—the Tower with its thousand years of history, ancient customs, and tame, resident ravens—the only reminder that at various times right up to the nineteenth century a royal menagerie was kept there.

Tower Bridge, which is a comparatively recent structure, having been built in 1894, shares with the Houses of Parliament and St. Paul's the distinction of being among the most familiar of all the symbols of London. Sometimes the visitor who makes a river trip is fortunate enough to reach Tower Bridge when the great bascules, or arms, are being raised to let a tall ship through. The bridge, which is now too narrow for the volume of road traffic it carries, may eventually be pulled down, and a tunnel built under the Thames, but it will be a long time before anything is done about it.

Below Tower Bridge is Dockland. The London docks, spreading inland on both sides of the Thames, cover more than 2,000 acres, and there are about 45 miles of quays for the berthing of ocean-going vessels. But Dockland, which

The Tower of London and Tower Bridge with

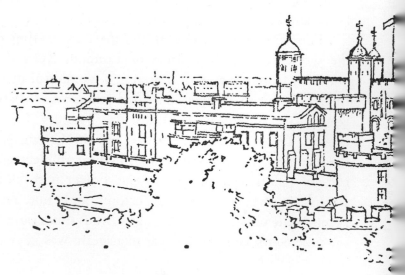

52

consists of twelve separate dock groups, all reached through "cuts" from the river, would need a book to itself. For the visitor there are special dock cruises.

It is in this stretch of the Thames, between Tower Bridge and Greenwich, that are found many of the most picturesque names and places of the whole riverside. Here are Execution Dock (where pirates and others guilty of crimes at sea or on the river were once executed); Gallions Reach; Wapping Old Stairs; Pelican Stairs; Cherry Garden Stairs; Elephant Stairs; and a number of quaint riverside inns, such as "Prospect of Whitby," some linked with the old smuggling days.

On the last lap of the voyage to Greenwich we sail round the Isle of Dogs, which, in fact, is not an island, and if it has any historic connection with dogs, this has

its bascules raised to let a tall ship through

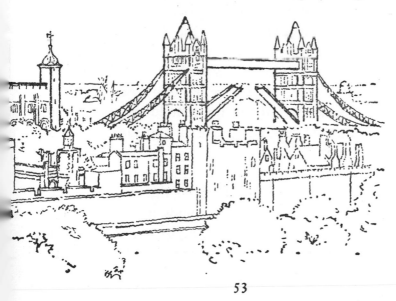

never been discovered. It is a part of the north bank shaped rather like a teardrop, round which the river winds in a loop. It is a fascinating network of docks, canals, cuts, road-bridges, and industrial areas. One of the best London bus rides follows the road round the bank of the Isle of Dogs, with masts and funnels of ships to be seen on all sides, and swing bridges, where the road opens to allow ships to enter the inner docks from the river.

And so, rounding the "cape" of the Isle of Dogs, we come to Greenwich, a long range of buildings of classical design on the south bank, with an imposing frontage to the river. The best place from which to see the white colonnades and the domed wings of the main buildings is a tiny park at the tip of the Isle of Dogs; the second-best place is a river boat rounding the "cape."

The buildings, which, as mentioned earlier, consist of the Royal Naval College and the National Maritime Museum, occupy the site of a royal palace built about 1437, which became a favorite home of the Tudor sovereigns. Here Henry VIII of the many wives, and his daughters Mary and Elizabeth (Queen Elizabeth I) were born, and here Edward VI died. The palace fell into disuse after the Tudors, but Charles II began the rebuilding, and in the present building the inspired hand of Sir Christopher Wren is seen once more.

We go ashore from our river boat at Greenwich Pier, where the little promenade in front of the "Palace"—for it still bears the old name in the minds of Londoners— always seems to have a holiday air, perhaps because it is a favorite place of afternoon leisure for the people of Greenwich, who like to sit on the benches watching the river traffic and looking across to the Isle of Dogs.

As we go ashore, the first exciting thing we see, in dry-dock by Greenwich Pier, is the *Cutty Sark*, the last survivor of the old sailing ships known as the tea clippers. This graceful ship, with her elegant lines and tall masts, is beautifully preserved and can be visited.

The Royal Naval College was originally a hospital for disabled sailors, so that Greenwich had its "Royal Hospital" as a counterpart to the Chelsea Royal Hospital which was, and still is, for old soldiers. But gradually the number of naval "pensioners," as they were called, became less and less, and in 1873 the buildings became the Royal Naval College for the higher education of naval officers. At the same time the tradition of providing hospital facilities for sailors has been kept up, and just outside the main

The Cutty Sark

gates there is a Seamen's Hospital, free to sailors of all nations.

Under one of the twin domes of the Royal Naval College is the Chapel, and under the other dome the Painted Hall, with a world-famous decorated ceiling. The National Maritime Museum occupies the Queen's House, designed by Inigo Jones, another great architect to whom London owes some of her finest buildings. It was completed for Henrietta Maria, the Queen of Charles I. This contains portraits, ship models, pictures of sea battles, and relics of all kinds, illustrating British naval history from Tudor times to the present day.

Adjoining the buildings is Greenwich Park, a fine, wooded open space climbing up a steep hill, at the top of which are the buildings of the former Royal Observatory. The Observatory has been transferred to Hurstmonceux, in the country about 35 miles from London, but the old buildings in Greenwich still stand on the imaginary line, known as the "Greenwich Meridian," from which East and West are measured on the surface of the earth.

If we climb to the top of the hill, so that the park and the buildings of the Museum and Naval College lie below us, we can, on a clear day, follow the windings of the Thames back toward the City and St. Paul's.

When we walk down again, through groves of magnificent Spanish chestnut trees, and past the children's playground, to the waterfront, to go aboard a river boat for the return trip, and when we take a last look across the river at the Isle of Dogs, we may recall that it was from Blackwall, on the seaward side of the Isle of Dogs, that three tiny ships—the *Susan Constant* (100 tons), the *Godspeed* (40 tons), and the *Discovery* (20 tons)—set sail on December 19, 1606, for Virginia.

And to our left, on the same side of the river as Greenwich, lies Rotherhithe, where, in St. Mary's Church, is buried Captain Christopher Jones, Master of the *Mayflower*.

Captain Scott's Discovery

IV.

SCARLET AND GOLD

When we made our trip down the Thames we started where the Oxford and Cambridge boat race begins. But there is another race held on the river, which is not only much older than the universities' contest, but is also an excellent example of how the colorful traditions of the ordinary people of London have continued alongside aristocratic pageantry.

This is the race for Doggetts' Coat and Badge, which was founded in 1715. Thomas Doggett, a famous actor of those days, awarded a handsome scarlet coat, with a great golden badge strapped to the arm, to the winner of a sculling race from London Bridge to Chelsea. The competitors are boys or men who work on the river, and the race is a severe test of watermanship over a very busy stretch of the Thames. It is still held on August 1st every year and, between races, the badge can be seen in the London Museum, Kensington Palace.

Another traditional river ceremony is the marking of swans to show who owns them. This is done by the Vintners (dealers in wine), and the Dyers, two of the City

Livery Companies that were originally established as associations of craftsmen organized for their common interests. They were called Livery Companies because they had royal permission to wear ceremonial dress, or livery.

The Vintners, founded in 1436, and the Dyers, founded in 1471, have royal permission to keep swans on the Thames, and every year, generally on a morning in late July, they start from Old Swan Pier, near the Tower of London, and work their way upriver, marking the swans. The Vintners cut two nicks on each swan's bill, and the Dyers cut one nick on the bill of each of their swans. This is known as Swan Upping, and all the swans unmarked are the property of the Sovereign.

These two ceremonies, the race for Doggett's Coat and Badge, and Swan Upping, are examples of how history and tradition play more of a part in the everyday life of London than they do in almost any other great city. It is true that other historic places, such as Florence or Siena in Italy, or Colonial Williamsburg, in the United States, hold annual festivals to commemorate historic customs, or keep alive a particular tradition by preserving buildings and relics and old-fashioned costumes, but only in London are centuries-old ceremonies repeated yearly, and sometimes even daily, so naturally that they are taken for granted as part of present-day life.

Every evening, for example, a detachment of guardsmen—soldiers of one of the regiments of the Queen's Foot Guards—marches from Buckingham Palace through Westminster and the City to the Bank of England for guard duty, and it is their special privilege to march through the streets of London with fixed bayonets, a privilege never otherwise granted to troops in the capital except during a ceremonial parade after a war or on some similar very special occasion.

The custom dates from the Gordon Riots of 1780, when a mob, led by Lord George Gordon, and demonstrating against abuses for which they blamed the Roman Catholics in England, tried to take the Bank of England by storm. Ever since then military protection has been provided by the Guards. There is a stirring account of the Gordon Riots in *Barnaby Rudge*, by Charles Dickens.

Every day, at the Horse Guards in Whitehall, and at either Buckingham Palace or St. James's Palace, depending on where the Queen's standard is flying, there is a ceremonial Changing of the Guard. At the Horse Guards, against a background of silver-gray stone and somber archways, the Queen's Household Cavalry— either the Life Guards with white plumed helmets, flashing steel breastplates, and scarlet cloaks, or the Royal Horse Guards, with blue cloaks and red plumes—mounted on magnificent horses, carry out, with breathtaking precision and the swift gleam of swords, the replacement of one detachment of mounted sentries by another.

At Buckingham Palace or St. James's, men from other regiments of the Brigade of Guards carry out a similar ceremony on foot, according to an elaborate and perfectly timed routine.

But by far the most impressive of all these displays of scarlet, or blue, and gold is undoubtedly the annual ceremonial of Trooping the Colour. This is held on the Horse

Guards' Parade to mark the Sovereign's "official" birthday. For this purpose, a special day is arranged in June—a month chosen because it sometimes produces very fine weather in England—irrespective of the actual birth date of the reigning monarch.

The Horse Guards' Parade is a great square between Whitehall and St. James's Park, flanked on three sides by offices of the Admiralty, or Navy Department, and the Army, and on the fourth side by the park. Each year the color (regimental flags and standards) of one of the five regiments of Foot Guards is "trooped" before the Sovereign. The five regiments are the Grenadier Guards, the Coldstream Guards, the Scots Guards, the Irish Guards, and the Welsh Guards. These are distinguishable not only by their cap bands and cap badges or the small plumes at the side of the great black bearskin headgear they sometimes wear, but also, even when they are in khaki, by the arrangements of the buttons on their tunics.

In front of privileged spectators in special stands, and great crowds of the general public lined up on the park side of the parade grounds, the Guards form a huge hollow square round the Sovereign, who sits as still and erect as the Guards themselves on a splendid horse, accompanied by military aides and officials. Then, to the music of the Guards' bands, the company whose color is being trooped performs a lengthy and impressive drill of marching and counter-marching, mainly to the solemn tempo of the Guards' famous slow march.

And when—as happens quite often in London, to many people's surprise—the day is fine and the sun is shining, Trooping the Colour (*never*, for some curious, traditional reason "the Trooping of the Colour") is undoubtedly one of the finest spectacles in the world. The brilliant uniforms and precise drill movements; the splendor of the setting and the colorful, ceremonial dress of the foreign Military Attachés; the stirring music of the massed bands; the fine procession of the Sovereign and the Guards from Buckingham Palace down that great royal avenue, the Mall, to the parade ground, and back again— all these combine to make a truly memorable occasion.

Another annual event that helps to make London an unrivaled center of free public spectacles is the Lord Mayor's Show, which is held in November. It originated in the thirteenth century when the Lord Mayor went from the City to Westminster to submit a list of "livery-

Trooping the Colour at

men," or City officials, for the approval of the King. It began, also, as one of the stately river processions in lavishly decorated barges which made the Thames in olden times the center of London's royal and official activities. In 1856 it became a street instead of a river show.

Today the procession makes its way slowly from the Mansion House, the Lord Mayor's official residence, by way of St. Paul's, Ludgate Hill, and Fleet Street, to the Law Courts, and the most fortunate visitors are those who have a friend in one of the Fleet Street newspaper offices, overlooking the route.

In this ceremony, scarlet, gold, and purple are provided by the Royal Life Guards' or Royal Horse Guards' mounted band and the Lord Mayor's coach. The mounted bandsmen, with their curious jockey caps, handsome uni-

the Horse Guards' Parade

The Lord Mayor's coach and (below) his coachman

forms, gleaming trumpets, and heavily decorated drums slung across their horses, wear superb purple riding cloaks.

The Lord Mayor's coach, which forms the climax of the procession, is a huge, gilded, horse-drawn carriage in

the care of the Lord Mayor's Coachman, a resplendent figure who catches the eye of children in the crowds much more readily than the Lord Mayor himself, almost hidden in the interior of the vast, ornate vehicle.

The rest of the procession is usually designed to illustrate a special theme—sometimes the Defence Services, sometimes the profession or trade of the new Lord Mayor. It consists of a large number of elaborately staged tableaux on floats, interspersed with detachments of

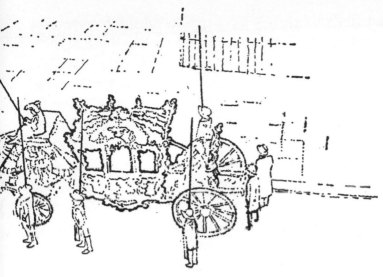

soldiers, sailors, airmen, policemen, and Service bands.

The Lord Mayor is chosen every year by the livery-men of the City Companies. The first recorded holder of the office was Henry FitzAlwyn, who was elected about 1192, although in those days the title was simply "Mayor."

Perhaps the best known of the early Mayors was Richard Whittington, who was elected four times between 1396 and 1419. He is the subject of one of the most popular of all English children's stories (equally popular with American children), and of the favorite Christmas "pantomime" called *Dick Whittington*, a traditional, elab-orate stage spectacle with music, comedy, topical songs, and wonderful transformation scenes.

The story—part fact and part legend—as you prob-ably know, tells of a poor boy who journeyed to London from the West of England because he had heard that the streets of the capital were "paved with gold." He was employed as a kitchen boy by a rich merchant, to whom he loaned his favorite cat for one of his trading ships.

Dick Whittington, ill-treated by the cook, ran away, but while resting on Highgate Hill, in north London, heard Bow Bells—the bells of the church of St. Mary-le-Bow—and imagined they said "Turn again, Whittington, thrice Lord Mayor of London." He returned to find that the cat he had loaned to his master for one of his ships had been bought for a fabulous sum of money by a foreign king whose palace was overrun with rats, so Dick, now rich, married his master's daughter and eventually became "thrice Lord Mayor of London."

This legend appears to have been first recorded about 1605. There was a real Richard Whittington, a draper who flourished in London at the end of the fourteenth and the beginning of the fifteenth centuries, and who was Lord Mayor four, not merely three, times. And to this day there is a stone by the side of the road on Highgate Hill still known as the "Whittington Stone," where Dick is said to have been resting when he heard the bells.

The Whittington Stone

66

Today the office of Lord Mayor is still one of great dignity and importance. The holder is always a man of high standing in the City, and he is usually wealthy, so as to be able to meet the heavy expenses of his year of office. In the City he ranks next to the Sovereign, and traditionally, as we have seen, the Sovereign must ask his permission before entering the City.

The Lord Mayor is also Chief Magistrate of the City, first Justice of the Central Criminal Court (the Old Bailey), Admiral of the Port of London, and a Trustee of St. Paul's Cathedral.

Magnificent horse-drawn carriages are, of course, a well-known feature of London's pageantry, as they are used for the Coronation, royal weddings, State drives, the State opening of Parliament, and sometimes for distinguished foreign visitors. And there is an undoubted revival of interest in the river as a processional way; the Queen has taken guests in the Royal Barge down the river to Greenwich.

There are many other examples of time-honored ceremonial, each with its colorful trappings of dress and language. Some are carried out in public, others can be watched if application is made in writing beforehand.

Every evening in the Tower of London, when the gates are closed, the keys are surrendered to the Resident Governor, and a tour is made of all the sentry posts, where the challenge is made: "Who goes there?" and the answer is given: "The King's (or Queen's) keys."

When the Law Courts reopen for the term that begins in October, the Judges and members of the Bar attend a

A Judge in traditional wig and gown

special service in Westminster Abbey, and afterwards enter the Courts in procession, wearing the traditional wigs and gowns of their calling.

We have already noticed the Chelsea Pensioners in their handsome, scarlet coats: every year, on or near Royal Oak Day in May—which commemorates one of Charles II's escapes from his enemies—a special Founder's Day service is held in the chapel of the Royal Hospital.

And another yearly event is the searching of the vaults of the Houses of Parliament by the Yeomen Warders ("Beefeaters") early in the morning of the day Parliament reopens for the new session.

This, of course, is a reminder of the seventeenth-century "Gunpowder Plot," when Guy Fawkes (or Vaux) and his fellow-conspirators made plans to blow up the

Houses of Parliament, but the gunpowder and fuses were found in the cellars in time to foil the plot.

This is the event that English children look forward to commemorating on November 5th every year with fireworks and bonfires and grotesque effigies called "Guys" (for Guy Fawkes) which are burnt on the bonfires.

In addition to the great military spectacles, and the annual Royal Tournament, the capital's picked troops can often be watched on parade at Wellington Barracks, near Buckingham Palace, or "Beating Retreat" on summer evenings at the Horse Guards, or Chelsea Barracks, or the Royal Hospital grounds.

The grim, old buildings of Chelsea Barracks were recently demolished, and the new quarters for the Guards there are a showplace in themselves.

A Guy Fawkes effigy

CITY AND WEST END

If, like the Romans, we begin now somewhere near London Bridge, we can take a closer look at the two historic towns that make up central London—the City of London and the City of Westminster.

As mentioned earlier, the City covers an area of just over one square mile and is often described as "the Square Mile."

It is governed by the Lord Mayor and two Courts, the Court of Aldermen and the Court of Common Council, which sit in Guildhall—the well-informed Londoner never says "the" Guildhall—where also the Lord Mayor's banquets are held, and where the sovereigns and leaders of foreign countries are received when they visit the City.

The City has its own police force, quite distinct from the Metropolitan Police, who are responsible for law and order in the rest of London. If we look carefully, we notice that the City policemen have a narrow band of red and white stripes on the sleeve, just above the wrist, while the sleeve band worn by the policemen elsewhere in London has blue and white stripes.

The Square Mile is not only the oldest part of London, but it is also the financial center, like the Wall Street district of New York. Here are the Bank of England, the headquarters of the other banks, the Stock Exchange, the commodity exchanges, the shipping companies, and the British branches of the world's most famous finance and trading firms. The City, therefore, also means the center of the British money market, so that people talk about business being very quiet or lively "in the City," in the same way that Americans talk of things being brisk or slow on Wall Street.

Within the City have been found most of London's archaeological relics—fragments of Roman pottery and footwear, coins, and parts of the Roman wall. An impressive piece of the wall has been preserved close to All Hallows Church, which is near the Tower of London, and part of the City is called London Wall.

Leadenhall Market stands on the site of the Roman forum and it is not long since relics of a temple of Mithras were found in the City, and are being carefully built into the lower floor of a great new building.

The worship of Mithras, a Persian God of the Sun and Truth, was the last Asian religion observed in Rome before the establishment of Christianity. In some ways it resembled Christianity, and it became popular with the Roman soldiers, who brought it to Britain.

St. Paul's Cathedral, on the other hand, the crowning glory of the City, which stands on a commanding site at the top of Ludgate Hill, was once believed to occupy the ground dedicated by the Romans to the goddess Diana.

A view of St. Paul's Cathedral from the Thames River

Sir Christopher Wren, whose masterpiece the cathedral is, repudiated this belief, and certainly no conclusive evidence has yet been produced.

Built after the Great Fire of 1666 to replace Old St. Paul's, which had a 460-foot spire, Wren's cathedral cost about $2,250,000, most of which was raised by a tax on sea-borne coal entering London. One result of this method of financing it was that the Lord Mayor, in addition to the Archbishop of Canterbury and the Bishop of London, became a trustee of the church.

Ever since bombs and fire laid waste to great areas around St. Paul's in the Second World War, arguments have been going on about the best arrangements of the new buildings, but on one point there is, on the whole, agreement. That is that however much London is modernized with superb, sky-reaching structures, care must be taken not to shut St. Paul's inside a great prison of steel and concrete boxes.

The war damage threw open entirely new vistas of the great cathedral, but at the same time, by destroying many of the nearby, narrow streets, made many people forget that although St. Paul's was crowded and cluttered, it was neither boxed-in nor hidden. The last time there had been a great deal of rebuilding was after the Great Fire of 1666, and this largely followed the lines of the narrow, medieval lanes and courtyards.

Without today's mechanical and technical equipment, the old builders were compelled to keep their cities fairly close to the human scale. Most of the houses, shops, churches, streets, and public buildings, though some of them were impressive, were not so vast or so high as to reduce the people who used them to the proportions of ants.

Against this modest background one or two superb structures—temples, cathedrals, palaces, government buildings—crowned and dominated the general picture. In this way the lovely skylines of old London grew, with St. Paul's dome and the nearby spires of dozens of smaller Wren churches. In just this way, the skylines of other ancient cities, such as Oxford, Florence, Rome, and many others, grew.

But now it is comparatively easy to build fantastically high, fantastically huge, office buildings, and there is a great demand for them. If these are placed without care for the general character of an old city, there is a great danger that they will change it from a wonderful human

73

St. Paul's Cathedral dominates the skyline

creation into a mere working prison for human beings.

This is a very great problem in London today, and although nobody wants to prevent the modernizing of the city merely for the sake of the old buildings, a great deal of thought is being given to the question of controlling the new developments so as to preserve what is valuable in the character of the old.

It is particularly interesting, therefore, for the visitor

74

to have a look, in almost any of London's public libraries, at the various plans that have been drawn up, and at photographs of the models that have been made for the rebuilding of the area around St. Paul's, and to wonder which of them will eventually be carried out.

For St. Paul's occupies a place in English life comparable only to that held by Westminster Abbey. Britain, the Commonwealth, and their allies—both American and European—have long turned to the great cathedral on the hill as a source of courage in adversity and a place of thanksgiving for safe survival. The scarlet and gold and ermine of coronations and royal weddings may belong to Westminster Abbey, but St. Paul's, the cathedral church of London, is where the ordinary people go to gather strength in those testing times which are as old as mankind itself.

Before leaving the City for the West End it is worth while having a final look at the Square Mile from the Stone Gallery, which runs around the exterior of the base of the dome of St. Paul's or, better still, from the Golden Gallery which is on top of the dome, at the base of the lantern. On the way up—by stairs only— there is the Whispering Gallery, which runs around the interior of the lower dome.

The lower dome, or inner cupola, is 218 feet above the ground, and is the one seen from inside the cathedral. The inner dome is made of brick, the outer dome of wood covered with lead. The total height from the ground to the top of the cross above the dome is 365 feet.

The Whispering Gallery, from which there is an ex-

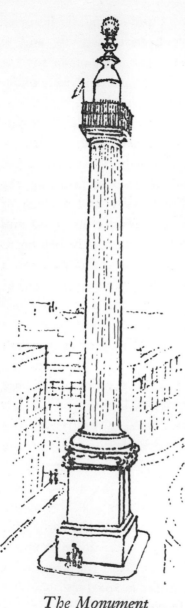

The Monument

cellent view of the interior of the cathedral, and of the decorations on the inside of the dome, is famous because, it is said, if you put your head close to the wall and whisper something, it can be clearly heard on the other side of the gallery. I once tried it, but it did not work very well.

The Stone Gallery, on the other hand, always lives up to its reputation, as the views from it are superb. And as we look east and west across the City, and up the river over Westminster, we can see that many more magnificent vantage points have risen above London since St. Paul's dome was practically alone in its eminence.

The nearest, apart from the brand-new office buildings around the cathedral, which have not yet become familiar, is the Monument, which was built from designs by Wren at the time the cathedral was being built. This

76

fluted Doric column, which, with the gilt urn surrounded by sculptured frames at the top, is 202 feet high, commemorates the Great Fire, which broke out on September 2, 1666, in Pudding Lane, said to be exactly 202 feet from the Monument. The fire ended at Pie Corner.

There is a winding staircase inside the Monument leading to the viewing platform at the top.

The Monument is east of St. Paul's, and if we walk around the Stone Gallery to the west side, the other high points for viewing London, both old and new, are in front of us.

Of the older ones, the best is, perhaps, the campanile or bell-tower of Westminster Roman Catholic Cathedral near Victoria station, a Byzantine-type building of red brick and gray Portland stone. The campanile, opened in 1903, and known as St.

Westminster Cathedral, St. Edward's Tower

Edward's Tower, is 284 feet high, and there is an elevator.

On the north of the Thames, in Bloomsbury, is the towering Senate House of the University of London, which can be visited on application, but the two newest and most impressive of all vantage points are the Viewing Gallery of the new Shell Building behind the Royal Festival Hall on the south bank (351 feet) (see page 26), and, highest of all so far, the new Vickers Building at Millbank, near the Houses of Parliament, which is 387 feet high—30 feet higher than St. Paul's, and 60 feet higher than the clock tower of the Houses of Parliament. (See picture on page 11.)

And for panoramic views there is Primrose Hill (219 feet), which has a diagram set in stone at the highest point, indicating the principal landmarks that can be seen, and the road along the ridge of Hampstead Heath just above the Vale of Health, from which there is a fine view from a height of over 400 feet.

The summit of Primrose Hill is also notable as the meeting place of Britain's present-day Druids. These devoted followers of the prehistoric Druids, who were believed to have met at the great stone circle of Stonehenge to greet the sun, join in a circle of white-robed figures every year to celebrate the autumn equinox by scattering apples and grapes on the grass.

From both of these points the whole of central London is spread out below, with the Surrey hills rising gently in the southern distance, and on a fine clear day it is fun to pick out the famous buildings and to try to trace the winding course of the hidden Thames.

But it is time now to descend the stairs from the Stone Gallery of St. Paul's, and to leave the great cathedral, which shares with Westminster Abbey the memorials to Britain's great men and heroes, and to make our way toward the western city.

There is still much within the Square Mile that must be left for another visit, but if, as we leave St. Paul's, we walk down toward the river before turning west, we shall find, in Queen Victoria Street, the College of Arms, or Heralds' College.

The college, which received its first charter from Richard III in 1484, deals with all questions relating to the armorial bearings of the titled families of England, and the tracing of their genealogies, or family records, going back hundreds of years. This is the place to which English-speaking people from all over the world apply if they believe they are connected by birth with some ancient English family. Many Americans have traced their ancestors in this way, and many have helped the work of the college. The splendid wrought-iron gates to the courtyard in Queen Victoria Street were presented to the college in 1956 by an American from Tennessee, Mr. Blevins Davies.

Merely to read the names of the officers of the college —the Heralds and Pursuivants and Kings of Arms—is like reading a book of medieval chivalry, yet they all appear, in the most matter-of-fact way imaginable, in the London telephone directory!

They are responsible to the Earl Marshal (a post held by the Dukes of Norfolk since 1672) for arranging ceremonies of State. The Earl Marshal also presides over the High Court of Chivalry, which still exists to settle problems that may arise over the bearing of coats of arms or other questions of hereditary nobility. And the college also advises newly created title-holders on their titles and insignia.

Our way westward lies through Fleet Street, running parallel to the Thames. On the left-hand side as we go toward Westminster is the Temple, which we glimpsed from the river, but this time we can enter it through Wren's magnificent gate of 1670 and explore it in detail. On the north side of Fleet Street there is still something of a rabbit warren of courtyards and alleyways, all winding and twisting and leading into each other.

Dr. Samuel Johnson's house, Gough Square

The Clarke-Hall bookshop, in Wine Office Court

Much of this warren was destroyed by bombs and fire, and some of the most impressive rebuilding in London has been done in this area, but there is still enough left of the old corners—Wine Office Court, Johnson's Court, Racquet Court, and others—to repay a visit. Particularly worth seeing are Dr. Samuel Johnson's house in Gough Square, now a museum, where the great dictionary-maker lived from 1748 to 1758; the old Cheshire Cheese public house in Wine Office Court and, also in Wine Office Court, one of the most delightful small bookshops in the whole of London, the Clarke-Hall shop, which is in a charming old house and has a unique selection of books on London, old-fashioned and rare children's books, and treasures of all kinds for the collector. (See pages 80 and 81, and also the picture on page 28.)

At Temple Bar we leave the City of London and enter Westminster, with the impressive, Gothic-style High Courts of Justice looking rather like a long, rambling cathedral or a turreted medieval château on our right.

The Strand, which, as its name indicates, was once a real strand, or riverside road, has the Savoy Hotel and Simpson's famous restaurant among its best-known features, but it also has, off a short steep hill leading down to the river, the Chapel of the Savoy, a little-known but most attractive gem of historical interest.

The chapel was built in 1505 on part of the site of the old Savoy Palace, which dated from 1245 and was the gift from Henry III to his wife's uncle, Peter, Earl of Savoy and Richmond. It is now the Chapel of the Royal Victorian Order, one of the orders of chivalry closely linked with the royal family, and is a private chapel of the Queen in her capacity as Duke of Lancaster (not Duchess, but Duke, because the reigning sovereign, whether King or Queen, is Duke of Lancaster). It contains an hour-glass by which Queen Victoria was said to time the preacher's sermon, and many other things of historic and artistic interest.

At the western end of the Strand, in Craven Street,

at No. 36, is the house where Benjamin Franklin (1706-1790), the American scientist and statesman, lodged happily with the kindly Mrs. Stevenson, and Polly her daughter, and Nanny the cat. And as Craven Street goes down to the Thames, we are reminded of how, one fine summer's day in the eighteenth century, Franklin swam most of the way from Chelsea to Blackfriars. But the river was cleaner and less crowded then!

The house where Benjamin Franklin lived

On the north side of the Strand, walking westward from Aldwych toward Charing Cross, we catch a glimpse of one of London's most famous old theaters, the Theatre Royal, Drury Lane, better known simply as "Drury Lane," where *My Fair Lady* has been running for years—and will probably still be running for years to come. (See picture, page 84.)

A little farther westward, we find ourselves in Covent Garden, equally famous for its great market and for its great Opera House, one of the most celebrated in Europe. (See picture, page 86.)

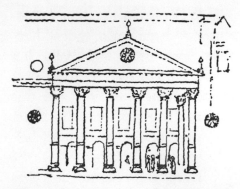

The Theatre Royal, Drury Lane

The fruit, flower, and vegetable market is practically wrapped around the Opera House, so close does it press on the magnificent theater. The fascinating pictorial contrasts provided at the end of a performance, when the crowds pour out of the colonnaded opera house entrance into the narrow streets, where the cars try to pick their way through the market lanes, still has much of the theatrical quality of the stage set in *My Fair Lady*.

The question of moving Covent Garden market out of Central London, where, of course, it snarls up the traffic, is one that seems to be a permanent topic in London life, and some day, no doubt, something will be done about it. In the meantime it is a wonderful place to visit, with fragments of the original Italianate piazza which once made it one of the most fashionable parts of London. There is also the little church of St. Paul, Covent Garden, which was designed by Inigo Jones and has its own tiny garden. It is known, because of its long associations with the theater in London, as "the actors' church," and is also linked with the centuries-old "Punch and Judy" entertainment for children.

The name of Covent Garden goes back to the convent garden of the parish of St. Peter's, Westminster, which, before the middle of the sixteenth century, extended from the Strand to Long Acre, the street which now forms the northern boundary of the market area. Toward the end of the sixteenth century stalls were set up for the sale of vegetables, and by 1631 a square was laid out, bordered on the north and east by a piazza, designed by Inigo Jones.

The area is now almost entirely occupied by glassed-in market halls, aisles of storehouses, and stalls open to the sky. Throughout the night great trucks converge on Covent Garden with produce from London's rail terminals or direct from the country around London—known as the "home counties"—and from farther afield. The market

Covent Garden market

is at its busiest toward morning, and the bars and public houses have licensing hours different from those in the rest of London, so that they can open for the market workers when most of London is asleep.

In Paris, one of the traditional ways to conclude a night out is with onion soup in Les Halles, the great central market; in London all-night celebrations often end with an early morning visit to Covent Garden market, where the scent of the freshly unpacked flowers, fruits, and vegetables mingles with the fragrance of hot coffee and freshly baked rolls to make a wonderful start of the new day.

The theater—the Royal Opera House, Covent Garden, to give it its full title—is the headquarters of opera and

The Royal Opera House

ballet in London, and is associated with Sadler's Wells Theatre, in Islington, north London, as the permanent, official home of these two forms of art and entertainment. Here at "Covent Garden" can be seen the world's great stars of opera and ballet. The theater, with its magnificent stage and superb red and gold auditorium, is a thrilling sight—above all on gala nights, when the Queen or some other member of the Royal family is in the flower-decked Royal Box. The theater-goer who is fortunate enough to find himself at the top of the stairs leading down into the famous "Crush Bar"—the splendid red and gold refreshment lounge—during intermission is rewarded with one of the most glamorous spectacles in Europe.

After the Strand, still heading west, come Charing Cross and Trafalgar Square. The square was laid out in 1829-1841 by Sir Charles Barry, architect of the Houses of Parliament, as a memorial to Admiral Lord Nelson, whose 18-foot statue is at the top of the 185-foot Nelson Column.

On the terrace wall, on the north side of the square, are marked the official standards for British measures of length, and on the south side of the square, facing down Whitehall, is a mounted statue of Charles I, the king who was executed. It was set up in 1675, and every year, on the anniversary of his execution at the end of January, his admirers still gather to lay wreaths and hold a brief ceremony.

From Trafalgar Square, Leicester Square and Piccadilly bring us to what is generally known as the West End—

Trafalgar Square with Nelson's Column in foreground

the district of shops, hotels, theaters, and all kinds of day and night entertainment.

Immediately to the north of Trafalgar Square, behind the National Gallery and the National Portrait Gallery and the royal church of St. Martin-in-the-Fields, and making short cuts between Charing Cross Road and St. Martin's Lane, are several curious, little alleys, full of fascinating small shops specializing in antiques, stamps, model railways, old prints, old books, theatrical and ballet souvenirs, Oriental ware, and Heaven knows what not. It is a most wonderful "bazaar" to browse in on a lazy afternoon.

About halfway along Piccadilly, still walking westward, we can turn south through the district called St. James's to look at the lovely old Tudor palace of that name (see page 18), and then across the Mall and St. James's Park to see Buckingham Palace and later Westminster Abbey (see page 17) and the Houses of Parliament, or else keep going west to the fashionable area of Knightsbridge and the mixed fashionable-and-Bohemian areas of Chelsea and South Kensington.

Pickering Place, near Piccadilly

It is in the West End that we see pavement artists and street entertainers, and the crowded street markets and cosmopolitan shops of Soho. One of the best ways to explore London, of course, is to find the places where famous people lived and worked. William Penn, for example, was born in a house on Tower Hill, near All Hallows Church, where part of the old Roman Wall has survived, and he later lived in Kensington and Knightsbridge.

If we visit the Royal Institution, in Albemarle Street, Piccadilly, we discover that it was founded in 1799 for the spread of scientific knowledge on the initiative of that extraordinary character, Benjamin Thompson (1753-1814) who was born in Massachusetts and became Count Rumford of Munich, and was described by the English historian Edward Gibbon, as "Mr. Secretary-Colonel-Admiral-Philosopher Thompson."

In the West End we must not miss Grosvenor Square, with the Roosevelt Memorial and the striking new building of the American Embassy.

And Soho market will send us in search of London's other street markets, of which the best known nowadays are perhaps the one in Portobello Road, Notting Hill, and the Caledonian market, now in Bermondsey.

But every discovery in London suggests other discoveries, and as the subject is inexhaustible, the best thing sometimes is to wander without plan, letting each "find" suggest another line of search, until—if there is time enough—we may even find something that has not yet been noticed or written about.

For American visitors, of course, London is full of

Shepherd Market, Mayfair

interest, even apart from what is sometimes called "Little America," in and around the Embassy in Grosvenor Square. We have already found links with Benjamin Franklin and Count Rumford, as well as with Harvard University. There is America Square, between Aldgate and the Tower of London, where an important fragment of the Roman Wall was discovered; Lincoln's statue in Parliament Square, and George Washington in front of the National Gallery in Trafalgar Square. (See pictures, page 92.)

We have already seen how blocks of apartment houses for poorer people are often tucked away in the heart of fashionable districts in London. Many of these are "Peabody buildings," named after an American philanthropist who wanted to improve the tenements of "the industrious

Abraham Lincoln's statue in Parliament Square (above) and George Washington's statue in Trafalgar Square (right)

poor" in the nineteenth century, and some of them are now being brought up to date in line with modern standards.

The body of George Peabody (1795-1869) lay for a time in Westminster Abbey, before being removed to Massachusetts. There is a statue of him behind the Royal Exchange, in the City.

And if there is time, during an exploration north of Fleet Street, to visit St. Sepulchre's church, near Holborn

Viaduct, the visitor will find there a colored engraving of the American Indian princess, Pocahontas, who saved the English adventurer, John Smith, from death at her father's hands. Captain John Smith (1580–1631) was "Governor of Virginia and Admirall of New England," according to an old inscription.

Princess Pocahontas fell in love with Captain John Smith, and when she was told that he was dead she married his friend John Rolfe, who took her to England, where she became a celebrated visitor, much sought after in the highest circles. The princess died of smallpox at Gravesend, a Thames-side town in the estuary east of London, and was buried there. This was 1616, when Pocahontas was only 21, and on her way home to America.

Royal Exchange Building

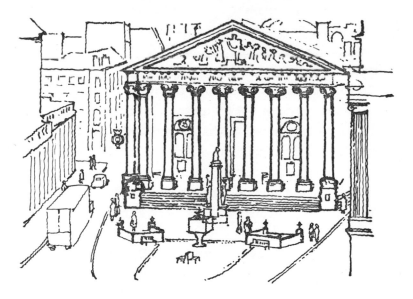

VI.

PLEASURES AND PALACES

There is so much to see and do in London, and so much going on all the time, that it is hardly possible to take a bus ride without making some interesting or amusing discovery.

Apart from the world-famous landmarks, such as Westminster Abbey, St. Paul's Cathedral, or the Houses of Parliament, there are many quaint and unusual things for the observant visitor to look out for, many little customs and events that have been part of London life for centuries, and still go on.

In Whitehall, for example—the wide street of government offices between the Houses of Parliament and Trafalgar Square—a plain but nonetheless quietly elegant, horse-drawn closed carriage comes bowling along among the great red buses and the cars. Driven by a coachman in a dignified, dark livery, it carries a solitary passenger—a royal messenger on his way between the Houses of Parliament and Buckingham Palace, St. James's Palace, or one of the other royal residences, with important documents.

In Piccadilly, center of the world of fine shops, hotels,

and exclusive clubs another picturesque horse-drawn vehicle can often be seen. This one belongs to Scott's, a famous and old-established hatter's shop, and is as smart as paint, with its immaculately groomed horse, elegant coachman, and decorative side panels with beautiful lettering.

In the City the messengers of the Bank of England wear tall hats and pink tailcoats as they go about their errands. During the school holiday periods we may see bareheaded boys in long, loose, blue coats, with leather girdles, white neckbands, bright yellow, knee-length stockings, and highly polished black shoes with buckles. These are the "Blue Coat" boys, pupils of Christ's Hospital, now at Horsham, in Sussex, one of Britain's great so-called "Public Schools"—which are, in fact, very private and very expensive.

The original buildings of Christ's Hospital, in the Smithfield area of London, have long since been replaced by extensions to the General Post Office and St. Bartholomew's Hospital, but another Blue Coat school, believed to have been built by Wren, survives in Caxton Street, Westminster. It has a charming figure of a blue-coat boy over the porch.

Scott's carriage

Another curious survival is the wearing of "pearlies" on special occasions by street vendors of fruit and vegetables.

Most of the street vendors, whether they had a little donkey and cart or pushed a hand-barrow, came from the east or south of London. Now called "barrow-boys," they were originally known as "costermongers," or "costers." The name probably came from the costard (custard) apples they sold, and the word "monger" for a trader is still quite common in England in such occupations as ironmonger, fishmonger, etc.

These Cockney traders, cheerful and high-spirited, were always glad of a pretext for a celebration, and one of their great annual outings was to the August Bank Holiday Fair on Hampstead Heath. This is one of London's best-known fairgrounds, with roundabouts, coker-nut (coconut) shies, sideshows, and every other kind of amusement. And for this special outing the costers used to appoint a "Pearly King" and a "Pearly Queen," whose clothes were covered from head to foot with pearl buttons.

There is a theory that this fashion began when a whole shipload of pearl buttons was salvaged from a freighter that was damaged in an accident and foundered in the London docks. Whatever the origin, it became a popular kind of dressing up, and a favorite costume of the Cockney comedians who were an outstanding feature of the English music-hall sixty years ago.

Occasionally even today, costers in "pearlies" can be seen in the West End of London, collecting money for charitable purposes, and their full "regalia" is still brought

Costers in "pearlies" in their decorated cart

out for the annual van-horse parade in Regent's Park, and, to a lesser extent, for, " 'appy 'Ampstead"—the fairground on Hampstead Heath. But the little carts themselves, particularly from south of the Thames, in Battersea, are as much a distinctive part of the life of London as ever.

How long this will go on, with the growth of supermarkets and self-service stores, it is impossible to say. But it is still possible, in Chelsea, for example, in the early morning, to see the little costers' carts, laden with fruits, vegetables, or flowers, come spanking over the Albert Bridge from Battersea, to sell their wares from door to door in the little streets by the river.

There is, too, another interesting point about these little carts. Most of them are gaily decorated with painted flowers and patterns—rather like the barges or "narrowboats" which ply their trade as carriers on England's canals. Some of them, indeed, are quite elaborately carved and decorated along the sides and shafts and back-board— a curious survival of the kind of popular art that gave us painted farm wagon's, ships' figureheads, gypsy caravans, horse brasses, and the carved and painted wooden horses of the carrousel.

*One of Pollock's
toy theaters*

Examples of all these arts and customs are to be seen, of course, in the London museums. One recent exhibition was devoted entirely to the "Pearly Kings and Queens," and will no doubt be revived from time to time. This particular exhibition was held in Pollock's Toy Museum, which is in itself one of the outstanding treasures of London.

The original firm of Benjamin Pollock was famous in the nineteenth century for its toy theaters. These consisted of sheets of scenery and characters which could be cut out and mounted so that children could enact popular plays of the period, rather like a simplified puppet show. Painted sheets were more expensive than those in black and white, from which came the expression "penny plain, tuppence colored," once familiar to all English children.

The original Pollock's "wholesale and retail Theatrical

print and Tinsel warehouses" was situated in Hoxton Street, Shoreditch, in the heart of London's East End. It was owned by Benjamin Pollock from 1876 until his death in 1937, when it was carried on by Miss Louise Pollock until it was destroyed in the bombing of London during the last war.

After the war a great deal of the original material was recovered, and Pollock's Toy Museum and Toy Theatres shop was reopened in a delightful old house, all stairs and odd corners, in Monmouth Street, near Cambridge Circus, in the center of London's theater, restaurant, and entertainments area. This combined museum and shop still exhibits, and sells, toy theaters, ranging from the simplest to the most elaborate, as well as lots of other delightful toys of many periods and many countries.

And the visitor who enjoys such places will also find it well worth while to go to Old Battersea House across the Thames. This is a fine old house, built about 1699, and may even have been designed by Sir Christopher Wren. In it the present owner has gathered together a remarkable collection of paintings, furniture, fine needlework and other objects of Victorian art, which can be seen on Monday afternoons on payment of a small sum to help toward the upkeep of the collection.

But unless we are going to spend months or even years in London we must not spend so much time exploring the odd corners that we miss the best-known centers of interest and enjoyment. We should not neglect, for example, the London Museum itself, where the history and growth of the city is displayed in models and pictures, with lots of exhibits from Roman times and earlier, showing what Londoners wore, and made, and cooked with, and what their children played with, throughout the ages.

The Museum is housed in Kensington Palace, Kensington Gardens. It was the chief private residence of the sovereign until 1760. Queen Victoria was born there, and apart from the museum, some of the State apartments can be visited. Parts of the palace consist of what are known as "grace and favour" apartments. This means that friends of the royal family are allowed to live in them as a special mark of favor. One of these parts of the palace was the first home of Princess Margaret and her husband, the photograper Antony Armstrong-Jones, who is now Lord Snowdon.

In addition to the interest of the museum, and the charm of the red-brick palace itself, there is another good reason for putting it high on the visitor's list on a fine day. Kensington Gardens, in which the palace stands, are as pretty and free and open a place to walk or play in as can be found almost anywhere.

With London's Hyde Park, of which it is really a continuation westward, there are nearly 640 acres of open parkland, with a great lake (the Serpentine), shady walks, formal gardens, playgrounds, riding paths, bandstands, and refreshment places, all in the heart of central London. And—unlike Paris—there are very, very few "Keep Off The Grass" signs.

Kensington Gardens not only contains the "Long Water," which is part of the Serpentine, but it also has its own Round Pond, a favorite place for model yacht sailing. Near the Dutch Garden, which faces the "Long Water," there is a statue of Peter Pan, the hero of the play by the British writer, Sir James Barrie. Peter, the little boy who did not want to grow up, is shown playing his pan-pipes to the small creatures, real or imaginary, with which very young children love to surround themselves. (See frontispiece.)

Kensington Palace is the only one of the royal palaces inside London that is open to the public, but there is another, only 20 miles from the center of the capital, which can be visited. This is Windsor Castle, which has been a royal residence for at least eight hundred years. (See next page.)

With its great central Round Tower, or "keep," its courtyards, battlements, moats, and lawns, it is one of the most romantic-looking ancient strongholds in Britain. The grounds and battlement-walks are almost always open, and some of the State apartments can be seen when the royal family are not at home.

From the walls there are magnificent views of Eton College, perhaps the best known of all England's great schools, and the Thames valley, and the Castle also contains the Queen's Doll's House, designed by a famous architect, Sir Edwin Lutyens, for Queen Mary, who was the grandmother of the present Queen. (See next page.)

Also in the country just outside London is Hampton Court Palace, now no longer a royal residence, although like Kensington Palace, and St. James's Palace, it contains "grace and favour" apartments. George II was the last British sovereign to live there, and Queen Victoria

101

Windsor Castle

opened the State rooms to the public. No summertime visit to London is complete without a visit to Hampton Court, which, with its superb buildings, its incomparable riverside gardens, and its general splendor, is undoubtedly one of the most beautiful showplaces in the world.

Queen's Doll House

First built about 1520, in the reign of Henry VIII, the palace and its grounds, stretching alongside the Thames at one of its prettiest spots, only about 11 miles west of the center of London, make a perfect setting for a day in the open, with the art treasures inside the palace as an added attraction.

Part of the huge group of

102

buildings is Tudor, with a fine gate-house, a bridge over the moat, and courtyards, in that curiously warm and lovely Tudor red brick which seems to soak up and store the sunlight, so that one has only to think of Hampton Court to think of high summer.

After Henry VIII, successive sovereigns added to the palace, and under William III (1689-1702) Sir Christopher Wren—how much that is beautiful in England is owed to that one man!—built the south and east wings, and the gardens were laid out in their present form.

Wren's part of Hampton Court, including the long frontage to the gardens, is a classical symphony in red brick and mellow stonework, with elegant windows, pediments, and decorative details in stone that are different in character from, but combine harmoniously with, the Tudor river-front of the palace.

Hampton Court

On the river side of the palace there is the Great Vine, planted in 1768, which bears an annual crop of about 500 bunches of fine black grapes. On the garden side, at the north end, is the Maze. There is a special trick for finding one's way out of this tangle of narrow paths between high hedges, but most people forget it as soon as they find themselves inside.

The treasures of Hampton Court are practically inexhaustible, but if time is limited there is one thing that should be seen, whatever else is missed. On the garden front, between the garden entrance and the Wilderness near the Maze, there is a long herbaceous border set against a warm red wall. To walk by that flowered border on a summer's day, with the palace on one side, and the gardens on the other, is to know what the Greek playwright meant when he wrote about "the apple tree, the singing, and the gold."

Of the royal palaces inside London which are not open to visitors, but which are great centers of attraction, Buckingham Palace and St. James's Palace are the best known.

Buckingham Palace—called "Buck House" by the Londoner who wishes to be thought a smart man-about-town or a member of one of the aristocratic clubs in the Piccadilly area—stands at the end of the Mall, the royal processional drive from Trafalgar Square which offers one of London's few "Parisian" vistas.

It is a huge and—many people think—rather dull building, with a courtyard in front, facing St. James's Park and the Mall, and a big private garden behind. It was mainly built in 1703 by the Duke of Buckingham, who named it Buckingham House, and was reconstructed by the architect Beau Nash for George IV about 1825. Since then many more additions and alterations have been made.

Buckingham Palace

It is the point to which the London crowds turn at times of great national trouble or rejoicing, in the hope that the royal family will come out on the balcony above the main entrance on the courtyard front.

The sentries who used to march up and down outside the railings now remain inside the courtyard, where the ceremony of changing the guard can be watched. The visitor can get a glimpse of the gardens from the top of the buses that go behind the palace to Victoria Station, and it will be possible to see the gardens, for the first time, from the upper floors of the new skyscrapers in this part of London. The Royal Mews, or stables, in back of the palace, can be visited.

St. James's Palace, whose fine Tudor red-brick gate-house can be seen if we look down the hill of St. James's Street from Piccadilly, is a most attractive complex of old buildings, rather collegiate in character. Visitors can wander freely through the various courts, but entrance to the palace is permitted only on rare occasions, such as an exhibition of gifts after a royal wedding. (See page 18.)

Henry VIII had a hunting lodge on this site, built in 1532. Charles I spent his last days here, and walked across the adjoining park to the Banqueting Hall in Whitehall, from which he then walked the few yards to his execution. William IV was the last sovereign to make his home in St. James's Palace, but part of the palace called York House was the home of the Duke of Windsor when he was Prince of Wales. In Friary Court the accession of a new sovereign is proclaimed. Although the sovereign no longer lives in St. James's Palace, it is still a royal residence, and the guard-changing ceremony is carried out there when the sovereign is not in residence in Buckingham Palace. The adjoining Marlborough House was the home of Queen Mary, and Clarence House, nearby, is the home of Queen Elizabeth, the Queen Mother. Princess Margaret lived in Clarence House before her marriage.

Apart from the royal palaces, the description of "palace" still belongs to the Houses of Parliament which are sometimes referred to as the "Palace of Westminster."

Of the old Palace of Whitehall only the Banqueting Hall, designed by Inigo Jones, remains. Long used as an Armed Services museum, it is to be restored for use as a government banqueting chamber. Opposite the Banqueting Hall in Whitehall, and nearer the Houses of Parliament end, is Downing Street, a row of modest, late-seventeenth-century houses, with eighteenth-century modifications, in which No. 10 is the residence of the Prime Minister and No. 11 that of the Chancellor of the Exchequer. Extensive rebuilding has been done to the interiors of Downing Street and the adjoining Treasury building.

In the middle of the carriage-way in Whitehall, almost level with Downing Street, is the Cenotaph, a memorial to the dead of the First and Second World Wars.

Kensington Palace and Hampton Court contain only two of the many and varied collections—historical, artistic, or scientific—with which the British capital abounds. The National Gallery, in Trafalgar Square, has one of the world's outstanding collections of paintings, with Rembrandt, Holbein, the Dutch schools, and the whole range of Italian painting magnificently represented. Behind the

National Gallery is the National Portrait Gallery, where all the great men and women of Britain's past can be seen as they appeared to their contemporaries.

The Tate Gallery—which we saw from the river between Chelsea and Westminster—specializes in modern painting and sculpture, and there are art treasures from many countries and many periods to be seen in the Wallace Collection, off Oxford Street; the Courtauld Gallery of London University; Dulwich Picture Gallery; the Whitechapel Art Gallery; and the Royal Academy of Arts in Piccadilly. And in the Bond Street area of Piccadilly are the commercial galleries and art dealers who have helped to make London one of the most important centers for art sales in the world.

Chief of the museums which rank as art galleries as well as historical or scientific collections are the British Museum in Bloomsbury, which, with its vast library of millions of books and manuscripts, is a unique storehouse of human knowledge and achievement; and the Victoria and Albert Museum in South Kensington.

The "V. and A." has lots of exciting things tucked away in it for those who like to dig around in search of what other people miss. For example, there is a little room devoted entirely to detailed model theaters, with great productions in progress, and special lighting for each model. And the V. and A. also has "daughter museums," or branches, such as the Bethnal Green Museum, in the East End, which specializes in dolls' houses, pottery, and costume.

Also in the East End is the Geffrye Museum, devoted

to furniture and the arts of the home from 1600 to the present day. It is a charming early-eighteenth-century building originally designed as almshouses or free lodgings for poor people too old or too frail to live entirely alone.

Other major collections include the Duke of Wellington's museum in Apsley House, Hyde Park Corner; the Commonwealth Institute, in South Kensington, showing the history and resources of the British Commonwealth countries; the Museum of Practical Geology and the Natural History and Science Museums, all in South Kensington, and the great National Maritime Museum at Greenwich.

And in addition to these there are many highly specialized collections dealing, for example, with Chinese art, military history, transport, public health, toys, Jewish art and history, and Britain's traditional crafts and trades.

One of the more exciting of the smaller collections is the Soane Museum, in Lincoln's Inn Fields, devoted to architecture and the fine arts. It is in the house Sir John Soane, architect of the Bank of England, had built for himself in 1812, and among its unusual attractions is a comparatively small room, full of drawings and pictures, in which the wall panels can be opened out and folded back, revealing more and more pictures, rather like a conjuring trick.

Although this room is only 13 feet, 8 inches long and 12 feet, 4 inches wide, the ingenious arrangement of folding shutters on the walls enables it to hold as many pictures as a gallery 45 feet long and 20 feet wide.

The Royal Albert Hall

London has no movie house, theater, or concert hall devoted entirely to programs for young people, but there is no lack of suitable entertainment. Children's plays of all kinds are given, particularly during the Christmas holidays, at the little Player's Theatre Club and the new Mermaid Theatre (see page 50). There are also lavish spectacular pantomimes in the big West End and suburban theaters, and throughout the year the Youth Theatre Company presents Shakespeare and other classics in London and the provinces.

The museums offer exceptional facilities for young people, and musicians of school age have opportunities to join local or national youth orchestras. The Robert Mayer concerts for school-children have long been an important and popular feature of London life, and two works by the famous contemporary English composer, Benjamin

Britten, *Let's Make an Opera,* and the medieval play, *Noye's Fludde,* are occasionally produced by local groups and during cultural festivals.

In London one may hear the world's great musicians at the Royal Festival Hall, the Royal Albert Hall, Wigmore Hall, and other concert auditoriums. Concerts are also given in the Victoria and Albert Museum, and, during the summer, at Hampton Court or in the lovely grounds of Ken Wood, between Hampstead and Highgate.

Ballet schools and groups abound, and although the standard required is very high and the competition very keen, the gifted child may have a chance to become a student at the Royal Ballet School.

The Children's Opera Group provides an admirable service in encouraging musical interests at an early age.

And then when we think of London Zoo in Regent's

In the London Zoo

Park, the great botanical gardens at Kew, the innumerable parks and playing fields, the river trips and Battersea Pleasure Gardens, the Planetarium, Madame Tussaud's wax works, the special exhibitions and other entertainments for children, and the help that the officials of all these places are ready to give, we realize that London, old as she is, is not as forbidding as she sometimes looks, and that she has a great amount of charm for all those, young and old, who are willing to take a little trouble to know her.

Kew Gardens

Westminster, Charing Cross, St. James's, Piccadilly, and part of Soho

1. Opera House
2. Covent Garden
3. Savoy Chapel
4. Cleopatra's Needle
5. Victoria Embankment Gardens
6. Charing Cross
7. Franklin House
8. St. Martin's in the Fields
9. Trafalgar Square
10. Scotland Yard
11. Cenotaph
12. 10 Downing Street
13. Horse Guards Parade
14. National Gallery
15. National Portrait Gallery
16. Eros Statue
17. Shepherd Market
18. Marlborough House
19. St. James's Palace
20. Clarence House
21. Queen Victoria Memorial
22. Buckingham Palace
23. Victoria Palace (Music Hall)
24. Westminster Abbey
25. Houses of Parliament
26. Victoria Tower Gardens
27. Vickers Building
28. Tate Gallery

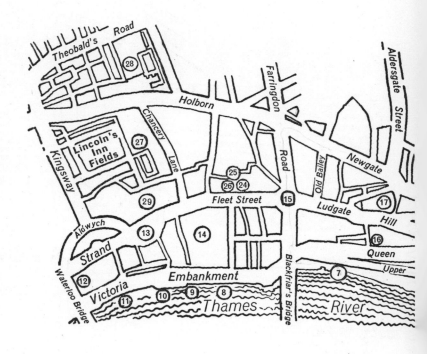

The City of London,

1. Royal Mint	15. Ludgate Circus
2. Tower of London	16. College of Arms
3. All Hallows Church	17. St. Paul's Cathedral
4. Custom House	18. Mansion House
5. Billingsgate Market	19. Leadenhall Market
6. Monument	20. Royal Exchange
7. Mermaid Theatre	21. Stock Exchange
8. "President"	22. Bank of England
9. "Chrysanthemum"	23. Guildhall
10. "Wellington"	24. Cheshire Cheese
11. "Discovery"	25. Johnson House
12. Somerset House	26. Clarke-Hall bookshop
13. St. Clement Danes	27. Lincoln's Inn
14. The Temple	28. Gray's Inn

29. Law Courts

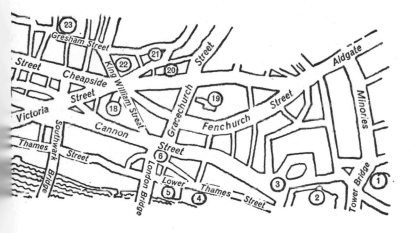

with some fringe areas

115

Hyde Park, Belgravia, Kensington, Chelsea, part of Bays-
water, and part of Mayfair

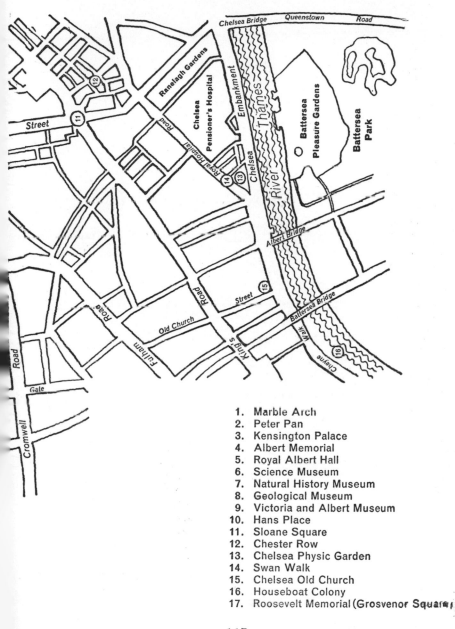

1. Marble Arch
2. Peter Pan
3. Kensington Palace
4. Albert Memorial
5. Royal Albert Hall
6. Science Museum
7. Natural History Museum
8. Geological Museum
9. Victoria and Albert Museum
10. Hans Place
11. Sloane Square
12. Chester Row
13. Chelsea Physic Garden
14. Swan Walk
15. Chelsea Old Church
16. Houseboat Colony
17. Roosevelt Memorial (Grosvenor Square)

117

1. Eros Statue
2. Globe Theatre
3. Drury Lane Theatre
4. Lincoln's Inn Fields
5. British Museum
6. Charles Dickens House
7. University College
8. Royal Academy of Dramatic Art
9. University of London
10. The Ivy, on West Street

Soho, Bloomsbury, part of Holborn

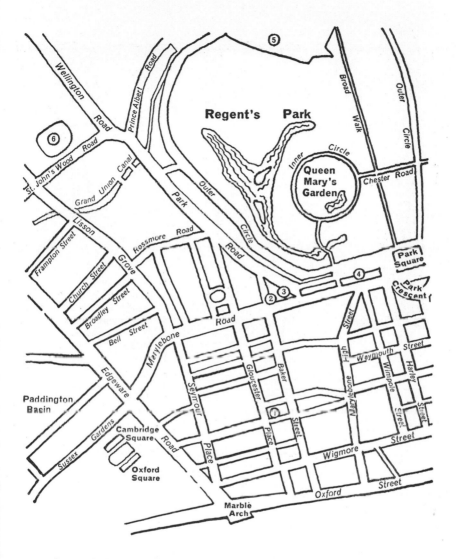

1. Courtauld Institute of Art
2. Planetarium
3. Madame Tussaud's
4. Royal Academy of Music
5. Zoological Gardens
6. Lord's Cricket Ground

Marylebone and Regent's Park

119

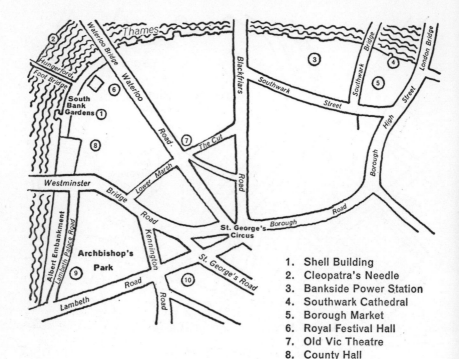

1. Shell Building
2. Cleopatra's Needle
3. Bankside Power Station
4. Southwark Cathedral
5. Borough Market
6. Royal Festival Hall
7. Old Vic Theatre
8. County Hall
9. Lambeth Palace
10. Imperial War Museum

Southwark, Lambeth, and Waterloo

INDEX

121

123

126

PRINTED IN U.S.A.

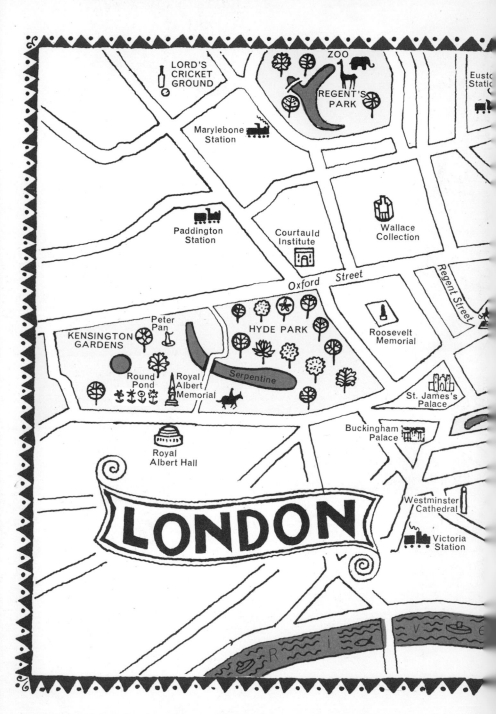